If your child struggles with a word, you can encourage "sounding it out," but keep in mind that not all words can be sounded out. Your child might pick up clues about a word from the picture, other words in the sentence, or any rhyming patterns. If your child struggles with a word for more than five seconds, it is usually best to simply say the word.

Most of all, remember to praise your child's efforts and keep the reading fun. After you have finished the book, ask a few questions and discuss what you have read together. Rereading this book multiple times may also be helpful for your child.

Try to keep the tips above in mind as you read together, but don't worry about doing everything right. Simply sharing the enjoyment of reading together will increase your child's reading skills and help to start your child off on a lifetime of reading enjoyment!

My Day

A We Both Read Book
Level PK–K

With much thanks to Sue Whitney

Text Copyright © 2002 by Sindy McKay
Illustrations Copyright ©2002 Meredith Johnson
All rights reserved

We Both Read® is a trademark of Treasure Bay, Inc.

Published by
Treasure Bay, Inc.
P.O. Box 119
Novato, CA 94948 USA

Printed in Malaysia

Library of Congress Control Number: 2002 103856

Hardcover ISBN: 978-1-891327-43-8
Paperback ISBN: 978-1-891327-44-5
PDF E-Book ISBN: 978-1-60115-500-9

We Both Read® Books
Patent No. 5,957,693

Visit us online at:
www.webothread.com

11-15

WE BOTH READ®

My Day

By Sindy McKay

Illustrated by Meredith Johnson

TREASURE BAY

I hear my clock ringing. My day has begun.

My day always starts with my good friend the . . .

. . . sun.

My mom says, "It's time to get up, sleepy head! It's time to get up and get out of your . . .

. . . bed."

I rush to get dressed. I know just what to choose!
I find both my socks. Then I look for my . . .

. . . shoes.

It's time to wash up—make the dirt disappear!

I take extra care when I clean out my . . .

. . . ear.

I run down the hall with my doggie named Tom.
We rush to the kitchen and both hug . . .

. . . my mom.

My mom gives me toast with the butter-side up.

She gives me some juice in my favorite blue . . .

. . . cup.

Old Tom likes toast, too. (He's a bit of a hog.)
But Mom gives him food that is made for . . .

. . . a dog.

My Mom says to hurry—there's no time to fuss!
I race down the sidewalk and hop on . . .

. . . the bus.

We head off for school—we don't want to be late!
Our teacher is waiting for us by the . . .

. . . gate.

She leads us inside and we sit on a rug.

She reads us a story about a . . .

. . . big bug.

We draw and we cut and we use lots of glue.

And when we use crayons, I always choose . . .

. . . blue.

At lunch I sit next to my friend Patrick Napes.

He loves to eat apples, but I prefer . . .

. . . grapes.

It's back to the classroom to learn this and that.

We learn about numbers and how to spell . . .

Cat

. . . cat.

The final bell rings. It's too loud to ignore!

I jump up from my desk and I rush out . . .

. . . the door.

The bus picks me up. We drive right by a lake!
At home waiting for me is milk and some . . .

. . . cake.

I play with my toys and watch TV a tad.

I hear a car coming! I know it's . . .

. . . my dad.

We're hungry for dinner. We help as we're able.

My Dad carries food out, and I set the…

. . . table.

It's time for my bath. Here I go! Rub-a-dub!

Dad turns on the water and fills up . . .

. . . the tub.

The sun has gone down now. Mom peeks in to look.

I'm ready for bed—after we read . . .

. . . a book.

Mom tucks me in tight and I'll be asleep soon.

My day always ends with my good friend . . .

. . . the moon.

If you liked **My Day**, here are some other
We Both Read books you are sure to enjoy!

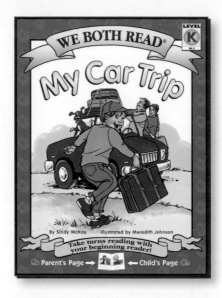

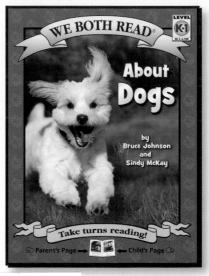